Muscles
and
Bones

JANE SAUNDERSON

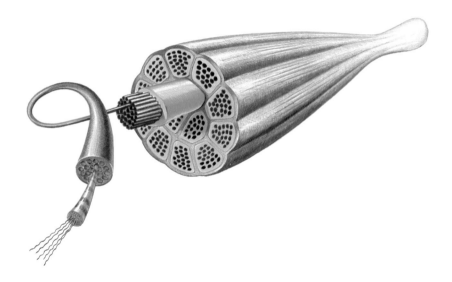

illustrated by
ANDREW FARMER and **ROBINA GREEN**

Troll Associates

Library of Congress Cataloging-in-Publication Data

Saunderson, Jane.
  Muscles and bones / by Jane Saunderson; illustrated by
Andrew Farmer & Robina Green.
      p.   cm.
  Summary: Describes the different bones and muscles in the human
body, giving their locations and functions.
  ISBN 0-8167-2088-6 (lib. bdg.)   ISBN 0-8167-2089-4 (pbk.)
  1. Musculoskeletal system—Juvenile literature. [1. Skeleton.
2. Bones. 3. Muscles.] I. Farmer, Andrew, ill. II. Green,
Robina, ill. III. Title.
QP301.S194   1992
612.7'4—dc20
                                                    90-42882

Published by Troll Associates.

Copyright © 1992 Eagle Books Limited

Edited by Neil Morris

Designed by COOPER-WILSON

Picture research by Jan Croot

Printed in the U.S.A.

10 9 8 7 6 5 4 3 2 1

Illustrators

Andrew Farmer front and back cover, pp 1, 2, 3, 6,
  7, 9, 10, 11, 12, 13, 14, 16, 17, 18, 19, 20, 22,
  22-23, 24-25, 26-27

Robina Green front cover, pp 4, 5, 21, 28, 29

Additional illustrations by COOPER-WILSON

Picture credits:
Colorsport 27
Science Photo Library front cover, 8 (top), (Frieder
  Michler) 8 (bottom), (Thompson/Stammers) 12,
  (Michael Abbey) 17

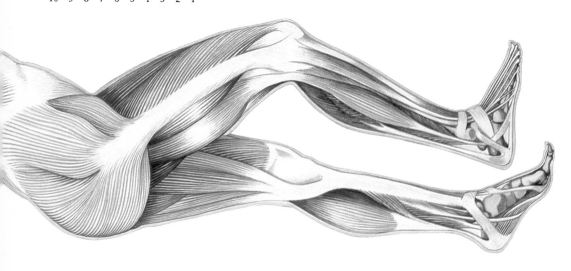

Contents

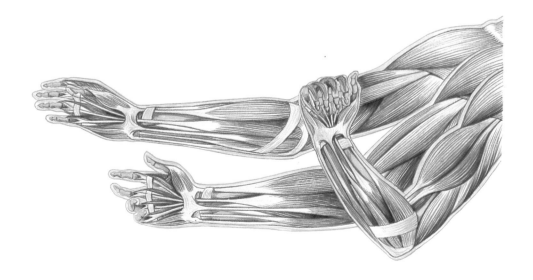

To live is to move

Try to sit as still as you can. Is anything moving? Even when you think you are still, parts of your body are on the move. Your chest moves in and out as you breathe, and during the next minute your eyelids will probably blink about twelve times. Some of these movements are under your control, but others happen without your thinking about them. You actually never stop moving – not even when you sleep!

Movement comes from your bones and muscles, directed by your brain and nerves. Together, they work like a remarkable machine.

But the body is more impressive than anything designed by people. It uses energy six times as efficiently as a car. It has run at over 25 miles (40 kilometers) per hour, jumped over 6 feet (2 meters) high, and thrown a ball at more than 90 miles (140 kilometers) per hour.

What man-made machine can grow and repair itself? The body can. Your bones make the blood cells that carry energy where you need it and help you fight infection. Exercising your muscles makes them stronger and helps to keep you healthy.

The body can also perform the most delicate movements, such as threading a needle or playing a guitar. Even a simple motion like turning a page is only possible because of bones and muscles working together.

Why you need a skeleton

Imagine what you would be without bones or muscles. Not only would you look like a blob of jelly, but you would not be able to move. An adult body contains about 206 bones, assembled into a framework called the *skeleton*. A baby starts life with as many as 270 bones, but as it grows, some of the bones join together.

Your skeleton is a living framework for all kinds of muscles and organs. Your bones provide a firm surface for muscles to attach to. Bones cannot move on their own. When you want to move, your nervous system stimulates your muscles, the muscles move your bones and you move.

Your internal organs are protected by your skeleton. Your skull protects your brain, as well as your eyes and inner ears. The nerves leading from your brain are protected by the spinal column. Your heart and lungs are guarded by your rib cage.

Your skeleton is also a factory and a storehouse for your body. Blood cells are produced inside bones, and then sent out into the bloodstream. Minerals needed by the body are stored in your bones as well.

You may think all skeletons are the same. They *are* very similar. But just as your face is different from your friend's, so your skeleton is unique to you.

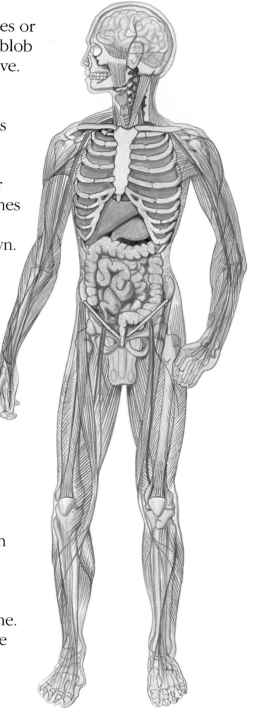

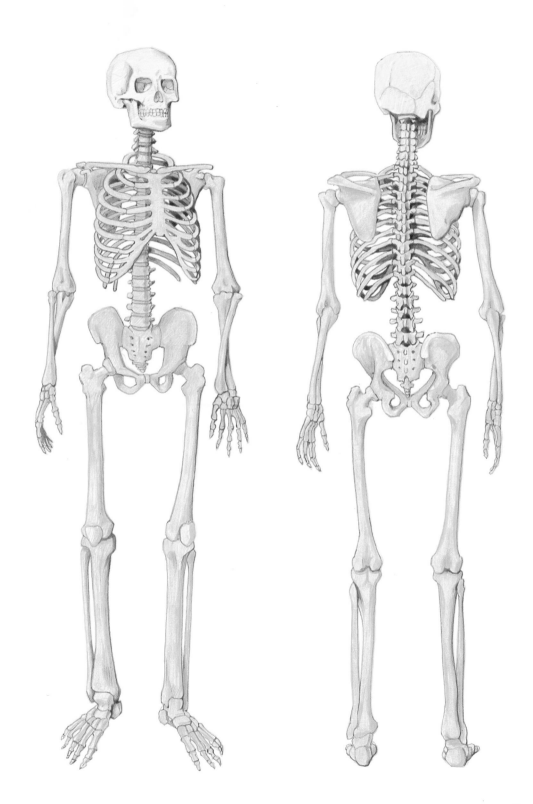

What bones are made of

Bone is four times as strong, in relation to its weight, as reinforced concrete! Each bone in your body has a special size and weight, and is designed for a purpose. Your largest bone is the thighbone, or *femur*, which accounts for over a quarter of your height. The smallest bone in your body, measuring less than one tenth of an inch (three millimeters), is the *stirrup bone* inside your ear.

A baby's bones are made mostly of a tough, stretchy substance called *cartilage*. Gradually minerals are added, and the cartilage hardens into bone. Bone is made of about one third living tissue and two thirds minerals. *Calcium* is the most important of these minerals, because it gives bones their strength and hardness. Let's look at a typical bone.

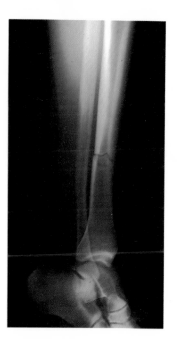

▲ Despite their great strength, bones sometimes get broken. This x ray shows the bones of the lower leg. The tibia, or shinbone, is broken about half-way down.

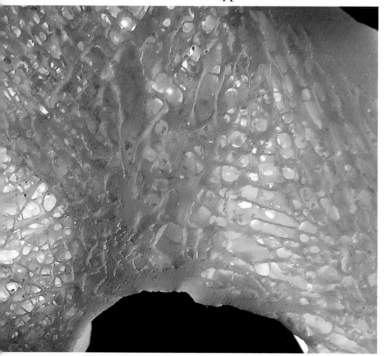

◄ Many bones contain hard, spongelike cancellous bone. This makes the bone strong but light. This photo shows the cancellous bone inside the hip bone.

1 The bone is covered by a tough skin, the *periosteum*. Blood vessels go through this skin to deliver the oxygen and food the bone needs.

2 The main shaft is made of *compact* bone, which gives the bone strength. Inside, it is hollow for lightness. If all your bones were solid, you would find it hard to move. In the hollow of the shaft is a soft, fleshy, yellow tissue, called *marrow*, which is a storehouse for fat.

3 At each end, the long bones contain hard, sponge-like *cancellous* bone. This gives the bone strength where it is most needed, without adding too much weight. Inside the hard, spongy bone is red bone marrow, which has the important job of making red blood cells. These cells carry oxygen and carbon dioxide around your body. Red marrow also makes some of the white blood cells that kill infections.

4 Where the bone's end forms a joint, it is covered in a layer of cartilage, so that it can move more easily.

If you break a bone, an x ray will show the broken bone ends. In order for the bone to heal properly, the bone ends are placed next to each other and then kept still. This is why we put a broken arm or leg in a cast. New bone tissue, called *callus*, develops and joins the broken bone ends. Gradually the callus hardens into compact bone.

Your skull, spine, and ribs

Your skull, spine, and rib cage make up 80 of the 206 bones in your body. Together, they form the *axial skeleton.*

The upper part of your skull is called the *cranium.* It is made of eight bony plates that have joined together. In a baby, they are not completely connected. When a baby is born, the bones are flexible enough to help it come into the world. The bones of the skull protect your brain, eyes, ears, and nose. Some of the bones at the front have air-filled hollows, called *sinuses*, which connect with the inside of your nose. These help to lighten your head and allow your voice to resonate.

Your upper jaw is part of your skull, while the lower jaw is the only bone in your head that you can move. This allows you to chew and to talk.

Your skull is connected to the top of your spine, or backbone, by a joint that allows your head to move freely. The spine is gently curved, making it strong and flexible, and it helps to keep you upright. It consists of 33 linked bones, or *vertebrae*, which get larger as they go down your back and have more of your weight to support. The vertebrae are separated by disks of cartilage, which act as shock absorbers. A tunnel runs down the center

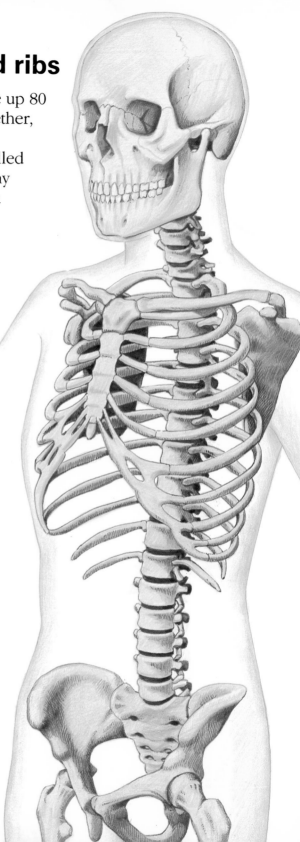

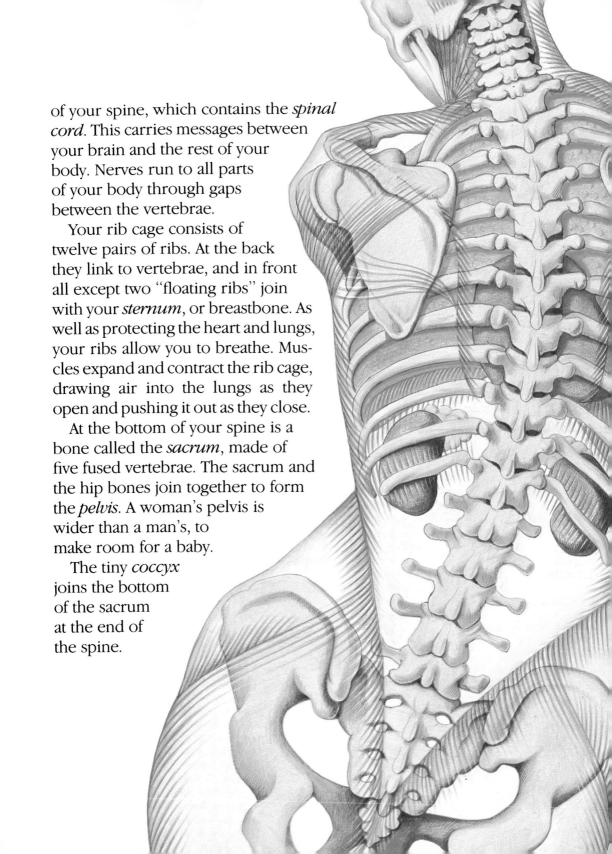

of your spine, which contains the *spinal cord*. This carries messages between your brain and the rest of your body. Nerves run to all parts of your body through gaps between the vertebrae.

Your rib cage consists of twelve pairs of ribs. At the back they link to vertebrae, and in front all except two "floating ribs" join with your *sternum*, or breastbone. As well as protecting the heart and lungs, your ribs allow you to breathe. Muscles expand and contract the rib cage, drawing air into the lungs as they open and pushing it out as they close.

At the bottom of your spine is a bone called the *sacrum*, made of five fused vertebrae. The sacrum and the hip bones join together to form the *pelvis*. A woman's pelvis is wider than a man's, to make room for a baby.

The tiny *coccyx* joins the bottom of the sacrum at the end of the spine.

Your arm and leg bones

The bones of your shoulders, arms, hands, hips, legs, and feet are known as the *appendicular skeleton*. The design of your arm and leg bones is very similar. But your legs must support more weight and move you around, so the bones are longer and stronger. Your arms need to be more flexible for reaching and holding, so their bones are lighter and more delicate. The large limb bones must be strong enough to cope with forces many times your body weight.

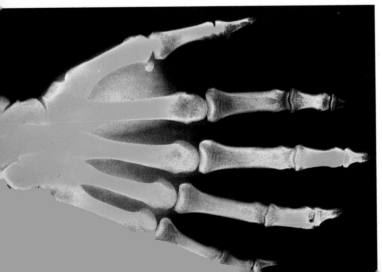

◄ A color x ray of the right hand. Eight small carpal bones make up the wrist. The palm of the hand is made up of five metacarpal bones. Finger bones, called phalanges, join the palm at the knuckles.

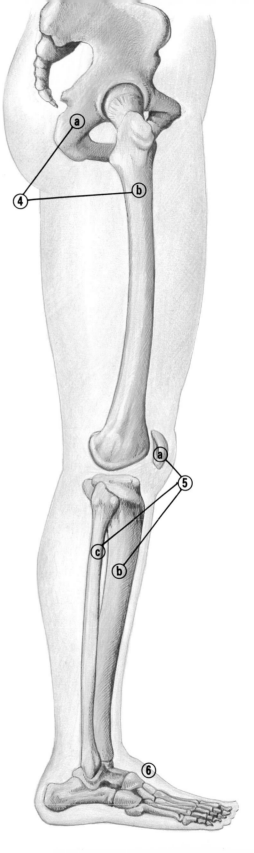

1 The shoulder blade, or *scapula*, is a large, flat, triangular bone. You have one either side of your backbone, lying on the rib cage. It is connected to the thin *clavicle*, or collarbone, without which your arms and shoulder blades would tend to fall forward. Find the top of your breastbone, and you can feel your collarbone running across to your shoulders. Powerful muscles support your shoulder blades and collarbones, and allow you to move them.

2 Your upper arm has one bone, the *humerus* (**a**), but to enable your hand and wrist to rotate, the lower arm has two bones, the *radius* (**b**) and *ulna* (**c**).

3 The 27 bones of your wrist and hand make them very flexible. Imagine how hard it would be to use your hand if you did not have a thumb that can move to touch each of your fingers.

4 Your pelvis (**a**) forms a strong girdle, to which your legs are connected. On each side, it has a socket into which the ball at the end of the femur (**b**) fits.

5 The joint at your knee is protected by the *patella* (**a**), or kneecap. Here the femur meets the *tibia* (**b**), or shinbone. The other, thinner, bone in your lower leg is the *fibula* (**c**).

6 The 26 bones in your feet form an arched structure. This gives you spring as you walk and jump. It also helps to cushion shocks as you land. Weight from your body is spread forward to the *tarsals* and *metatarsals* (your ankles and feet) and backward through one of the tarsals, the heel bone or *calcaneus*.

Different joints for different jobs

Our bones cannot bend, but we can. This is because we have joints where some of our bones meet. Some joints move more freely than others.

The joints between your skull bones, called *sutures*, allow almost no movement. These are also called *fixed joints*.

Other joints are designed to allow a little more movement, depending on the job they do. The joints in your spine are made of tough, stretchy cartilage. These disks give you a flexible back.

The joints that move most freely are those in your arms and legs. These *freely movable joints* have special features to allow smooth movement. The bone ends are covered in smooth, slippery cartilage. The joints are surrounded by tough capsules that produce lubricating fluid. This keeps us from creaking like a rusty gate when we move.

All these joints are supported and strengthened by tough, stringy *ligaments*, and by muscles.

If you sprain a joint, such as your ankle, the ligaments that support the joint become stretched, or torn. This makes the joint unsteady and painful. But if it is properly supported and only gently moved, it will heal itself in a few weeks.

Over a lifetime of moving, joints may begin to wear out. Bone ends can become brittle and cartilage less elastic. This condition is called *osteoarthritis*. It can make moving painful.

There are different types of freely movable joints:

1 Your hip joint is shaped like a ball in a socket. The top of the thighbone is like a ball and moves in the socket of the pelvis. Your arms and shoulders are joined in the same way. These *ball-and-socket joints* allow your legs and arms plenty of movement.

2 A special joint at the top of your spine, called a *pivot joint*, allows your head to rotate. The elbow also has a pivot joint.

3 Your knees and elbows have a joint that works like a door hinge. These *hinge joints* allow you to bend and straighten your legs and arms.

4 The bones of your wrists and ankles fit together like a puzzle. They glide next to one another as they move to form *gliding joints*.

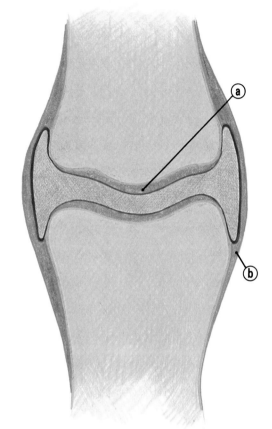

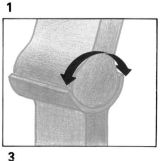

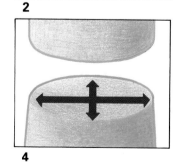

▲ The structure of a typical freely movable joint. The bone ends are covered in cartilage (**a**) to allow smooth movement. The joint is surrounded by a capsule (**b**) that produces lubricating fluid.

◀ These diagrams show how the different joints work:
1 ball-and-socket joint;
2 pivot joint;
3 hinge joint;
4 gliding joint.

What is muscle?

Your bones form your body's framework, but they cannot move by themselves. For every bone that moves, there are muscles to move it. About 620 muscles allow your body movements, and many more automatically control the movements of your internal organs, such as the heart and stomach. Muscles come in many different shapes and sizes. They make up more than a third of the body weight of a woman and almost half that of a man.

You have three types of muscle, each designed for different work:

1 *Voluntary muscle* is strong body muscle. It gets its name because you can tell it what to do. It is also called *skeletal muscle*, because it moves your skeleton, or *striated muscle*, because it looks striped under a microscope.

2 *Involuntary muscle*, or *smooth muscle*, is found in our internal organs. We have no direct control over this type of muscle, because it works automatically. For instance, it churns the food in your stomach as you digest a meal, and it allows your blood vessels to get wider or narrower.

3 The strong *cardiac muscle* found only in your heart is like a mix of skeletal and smooth muscles. It never tires, but just keeps your heart beating. If you live to be a hundred, your heart will beat over 3 billion times, and have pumped almost 66 million gallons (300 million liters) of blood!

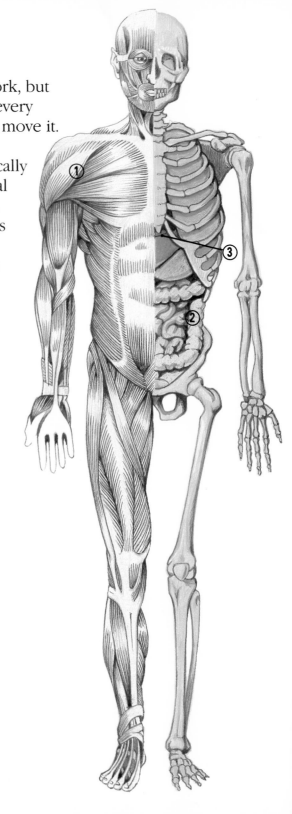

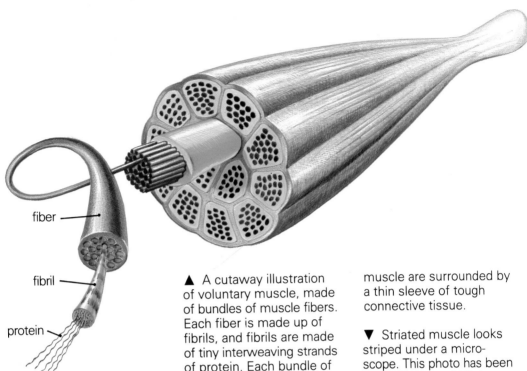

fiber

fibril

protein

▲ A cutaway illustration
of voluntary muscle, made
of bundles of muscle fibers.
Each fiber is made up of
fibrils, and fibrils are made
of tiny interweaving strands
of protein. Each bundle of
fibers and the whole
muscle are surrounded by
a thin sleeve of tough
connective tissue.

▼ Striated muscle looks
striped under a micro-
scope. This photo has been
magnified over 300 times.

A voluntary muscle is made of many thick
bundles of stringy *muscle fibers*. Each fiber is
made up of many smaller fibers called *fibrils*.
Fibrils are made of tiny strands of material that
are interlocked, like interweaving fingers. This
makes the muscle look striped. When the
strands move apart, the muscle gets longer, and
when they glide together, the muscle gets
shorter. Tiny nerves in the muscle control how
much and when a muscle lengthens or
shortens.

Many small blood vessels ensure that
muscles get all the oxygen and nutrients they
need to work. For your muscles to stay healthy
you must eat plenty of protein. All your
different muscles have one thing in common:
In order to stay healthy, they have to be used!

How muscles move you

Muscles are covered in a strong, thin "skin." The ends of this form the *tendons* that attach muscle to the periosteum of the bone. You can see and feel tendons on the back of your hand. These connect each finger to a muscle which starts near your elbow. Can you feel the tendons at the back of your knee?

Muscles run from bone to bone across a joint. When a muscle gets shorter or contracts, it moves a bone. Like a lever, the small movement of a muscle at one end of a bone may cause a much bigger movement at the other end. Because they can only pull, muscles tend to work in pairs. To understand this, let's look at what happens when you bend your arm.

1 To lift an object, the *biceps* muscle at the front of your upper arm gets shorter, bending the hinge joint of your elbow and raising your forearm.

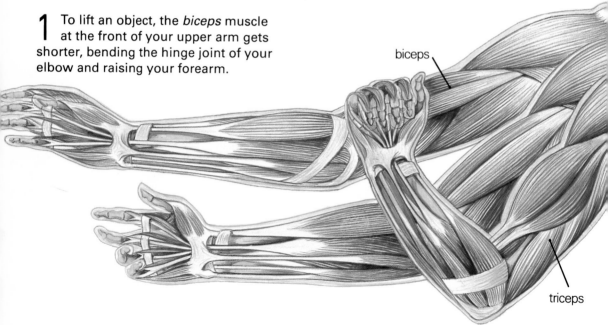

biceps

triceps

2 As the biceps gets shorter, the *triceps* muscle at the back of your upper arm gets longer.

To put the object down, the process must be reversed. Your biceps lengthens while your triceps shortens. This lowers your arm.

To feel these muscles at work, straighten your right arm. Now put your left hand on your right upper arm and slowly bend your arm. You will feel the biceps contract, getting fatter as it does so.

Many muscle movements are automatic and are called *reflexes*. A doctor may test your reflexes by tapping the tendon of the thigh muscle, just below your kneecap. This stretches the thigh muscle, which sends a message through nerves to the spinal cord. The spinal cord returns an instruction to the thigh muscle to contract. As it contracts, your foot kicks up in the air. By the time your brain realizes what is happening, the reflex is over.

Muscles sometimes cramp if they do not get enough oxygen. The lack of oxygen causes muscle fibers to go into spasm and contract violently. By moving and stretching the muscle, you can make the cramp disappear.

If you "pull" a muscle, you have torn a muscle fiber. Although this can be very painful, it will heal within a few weeks.

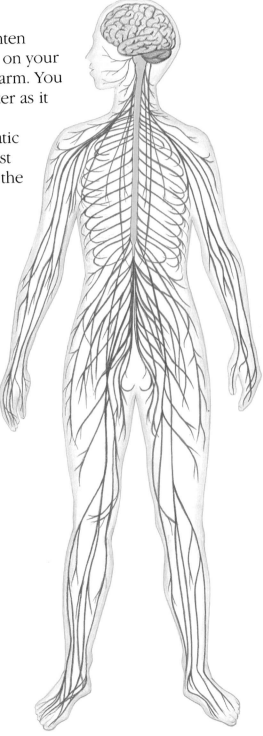

▶ Messages from the brain in your skull pass down the spinal cord in your backbone and along nerves to muscles and internal organs. Other nerves return messages through the spinal cord up to the brain.

Facial muscles

What's the first thing you look at when you meet someone? Usually it's the face. We use our faces to express our feelings. Sometimes a message is better expressed by a smile or a frown than it is by words. The constant movement of our facial muscles gradually forms the lines and wrinkles of old age.

We don't usually think about how we use our facial muscles. More than 30 small muscles run from our skull to our skin, allowing us to make many different facial expressions.

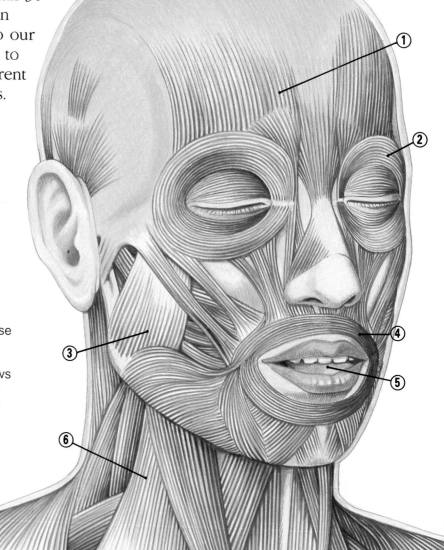

► Your nervous system has very precise control over the many fine, delicate muscles of your face. This allows for the great variety of facial expressions that you can make, from frowning to smiling.

1 A single sheet of muscle can wrinkle the forehead. This muscle also allows us to raise our eyebrows.

2 Muscles around your eyes allow you to blink about every two to ten seconds. So even while you are awake, you have your eyes shut for at least half an hour each day! Eyelids guard your eyes from injury, and blinking helps to keep your eyes moist and clean. The circular muscle around each eye enables you to squint or narrow your eyes to protect them from possible danger, such as very bright light.

3 Muscles anchored to the cheekbone and the side of the head help the jaws to bite and chew. Jaw muscles are so strong that skilled trapeze artists can hang from their teeth.

4 When you whistle, kiss, or talk, you use the circular muscles around your mouth. With the help of other muscles, you are also able to eat.

5 The tongue is a large muscle, and is capable of very precise movements. It mixes your food as you chew, and pushes food into the throat to be swallowed. You use your tongue, together with your lips and throat muscles, to form words when you speak.

6 The muscles of your neck connect your head to your spine, chest, and shoulders.

Trunk muscles

The central part of your body is called the *trunk* or *torso*. It contains all the vital internal organs, such as the heart and lungs. It also has the muscles that keep you upright and help you breathe and digest your food.

1 Your powerful back muscles help to keep you upright. Many different muscles running between the back of your head and your pelvis give your spine strength and flexibility.

2 A strong muscle called the *diaphragm* stretches from your backbone to the front and sides of your rib cage, supporting your lungs. As you breathe in, the diaphragm moves downward.

3 At the same time, the *intercostal muscles* between your ribs move them up and outward. This makes your chest larger, drawing air into your lungs.

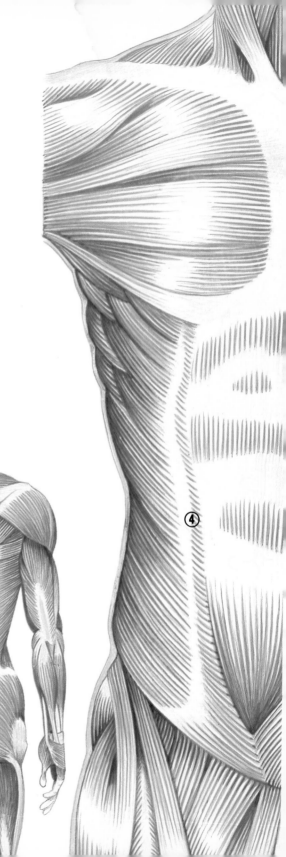

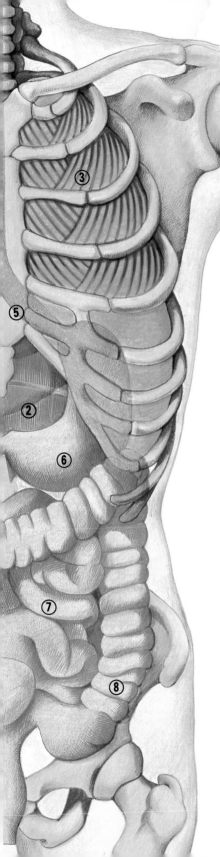

4 Three layers of crisscrossing abdominal muscles connect the rib cage to the pelvis. A fourth muscle runs like a strap down the front of the abdomen. These muscles make a firm but flexible protection for the stomach, intestines, and other organs.

Running through the trunk from top to bottom is a long muscular tube. This is our *digestive tract*, made of smooth involuntary muscle. The rhythmic contractions of the muscular tube gently move food through our body. We could eat upside down if we wanted to!

5 Swallowed food travels down the *esophagus*, or food pipe, into the stomach.

6 The stomach's three layers of muscles churn the food into a soup-like mixture called *chyme*.

7 After a few hours in the stomach, the chyme passes into the *small intestine*, which is over six yards (5 meters) long. The broken-down particles of food are transported into the bloodstream and delivered to where they are needed all over the body.

8 What's left of the food moves into the *large intestine*, and waste products finally leave the body.

In all, the internal muscles of the digestive tract work to move about 9 pounds (4 kilograms) of food and drink through over 8 yards (7 meters) of digestive system every day!

Arms and hands

Your hands are like tools at the end of a set of levers — your arms. Hands can make the most delicate and precise movements. Together, our arms and hands allow us to do all kinds of things. They will even support our weight if we do a handstand or hang from a tree. Watch a game of tennis and you will see how flexible the arm is. Watch a musician and you will see how skillful the hand is.

Layers of strong muscles surround the shoulder bones and suspend them from the back of your head, spine, and chest. These muscles help you to move your shoulders and arms. The *deltoid muscles* of your shoulders raise your arms outward.

Since arm muscles have their roots in your back, they have power for throwing and carrying. A javelin thrower needs the power of his whole body to get the most out of his throw. A weightlifter will not get far if he uses just his arms.

The muscles of your upper arm not only bend and straighten your arm, but also help you to turn your hand over.

You have 19 muscles in your lower arm. Together with the 20 muscles in your hand, these work your wrist and fingers.

The way that we hold things is made possible by the thumb. The power for grasping and holding things comes from your forearm muscles. If you clench and unclench your fist, you can see these muscles in action.

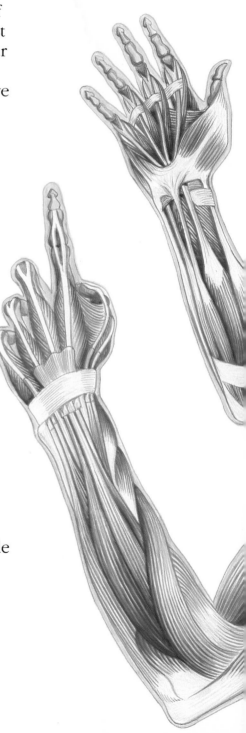

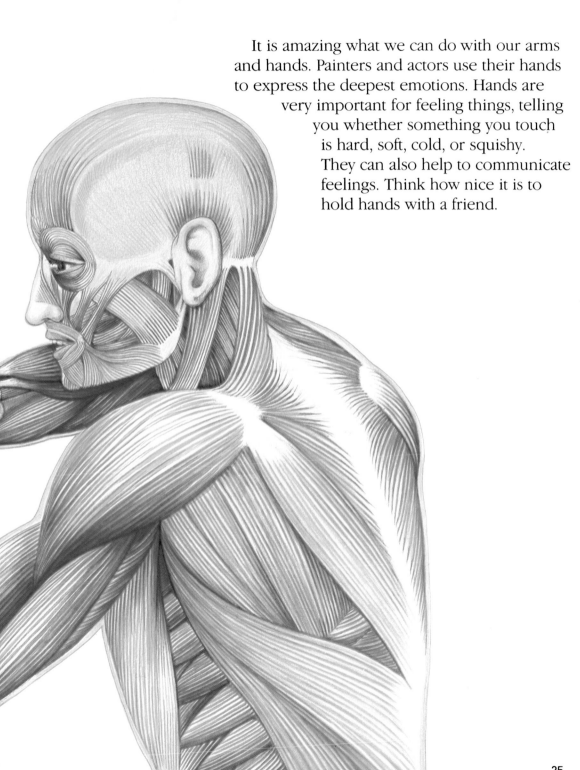

It is amazing what we can do with our arms and hands. Painters and actors use their hands to express the deepest emotions. Hands are very important for feeling things, telling you whether something you touch is hard, soft, cold, or squishy. They can also help to communicate feelings. Think how nice it is to hold hands with a friend.

Legs and feet

Your legs and feet can help you to squat, walk, or stand on tiptoe! They transfer your body's weight to the ground and help to move you around. Some of the largest and strongest muscles are in your legs, providing the power needed for running and jumping.

1 The strong thigh muscles are helped by the buttock muscles. Together they bend, straighten, and swivel your hips. The buttocks are among the most powerful muscles and are very important in helping you to stand upright.

2 Muscles toward the bottom of the thigh bend and straighten the knee.

3 The bulging calf muscle at the back of your lower leg provides the "push" that moves your whole body forward. It is connected to your heel bone by the *Achilles' tendon*. This is the strongest tendon in your body.

4 The ankles are surrounded by wide, flat ligaments. They encircle the ankle joints like bandages.

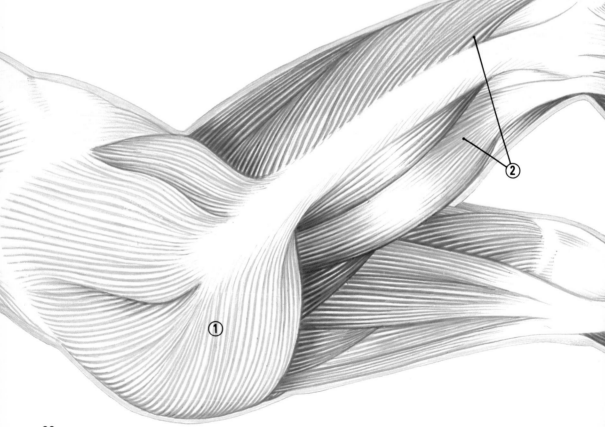

5 Your feet are full of small bones, bound by tough ligaments that make them strong. Many of the skeletal muscles that help you to bend your ankle and move your toes come from the top part of your lower leg. Their long tendons go across the front of your ankle joint and attach to the bones of your foot. When you put your foot down, the bones spread out a little. But as you lift your foot, it springs back into an arch.

In a little over two hours the world's best marathon runners cover more than 26 miles (42 kilometers), and their feet touch the ground more than 35,000 times.

▲ Through training, these marathon runners have developed strong leg muscles. To run well, their whole body must also be balanced and poised.

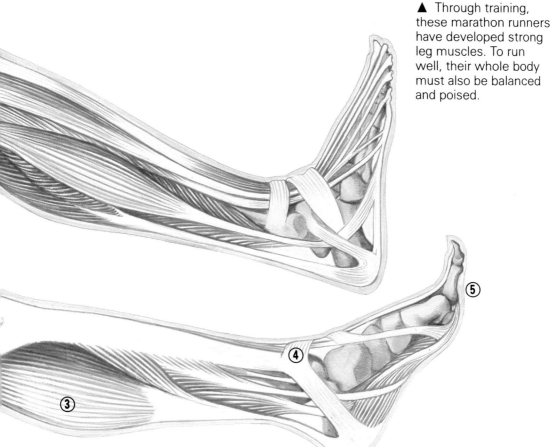

③

④

⑤

The way we move

Do you and your friends all walk in an identical way, like soldiers on parade? Do you all sit exactly the same way, like a row of robots? Of course not. Our muscles and bones, controlled by our brain and nerves, move us, but the way we move is unique to each of us. Most of the time we don't think about how we move, sit, or stand – we do these things automatically.

Sometimes the way we move puts an unnecessary strain on our body. If we feel tense, we sometimes pull our shoulders up toward our ears. This makes them stiff. Keep your shoulders relaxed, and let them rest lightly across your back.

We all have to carry things. How do you carry your school bag? The boy on this page is not carrying his bag very well.

Next time you are standing and waiting for something, see if you are standing evenly on both legs. Sometimes we lean to one side. If you do this, try balancing lightly on both feet. The old habit puts a lot of unnecessary downward pressure on one side of your body.

We are often told to put a lot of effort into things and to try hard. Sometimes we try too hard and use much more muscular effort than we really need for the job. Next time you are writing, see how tightly you hold the pen. Then put it down and begin again. Pick up the pen gently and start to write, using no more effort than you need.

Moving freely is not just for ballet dancers and gymnasts. It's for you, too.

▲ This boy has raised his shoulder, which may make him stiff. His spine is twisted as he carries his bag.

▲ It is better to put a bag's strap over your head onto the other shoulder. Then the load is carried more evenly.

▲ Or you can even the load by carrying two lighter bags, one in each hand, rather than a much heavier bag in one hand.

▲ A backpack is an efficient way of carrying things. The shoulders are open and the spine is not twisted.

Glossary

Achilles' tendon   the large tendon that connects the calf muscle at the back of your lower leg to your heel bone.

appendicular skeleton   the bones of your shoulders, arms, hands, hips, legs, and feet.

axial skeleton   the bones of your skull, spine, and rib cage.

biceps   the muscle at the front of your upper arm.

calcaneus   the heel bone (one of the tarsals).

calcium   a mineral that gives bones their strength and hardness.

callus   new bone tissue that forms to join broken bone ends.

cancellous bone   hard, sponge-like bone.

cardiac muscle   a type of strong muscle found in your heart.

cartilage   a tough, elastic substance from which many bones develop and which covers the bone ends in freely movable joints.

chyme   a soup-like mixture of digested food.

clavicle   the collarbone.

coccyx   the tiny bone at the bottom of your spine.

compact bone   hard, dense bone that forms the outside part of bones.

cranium   the upper part of your skull.

deltoid muscles   muscles covering the shoulders.

diaphragm   the large muscle that stretches from your backbone to the front and sides of your rib cage.

digestive tract   the long muscular tube that moves food through the body.

esophagus   the food pipe (upper part of the digestive tract).

femur   the thighbone.

fibrils   microscopic strands of muscle fiber.

fibula   the thinner of the two bones in your lower leg.

fixed joints   joints which allow little or no movement, such as between the skull bones.

freely movable joints   joints, such as the hip, knee, and shoulder, that can move freely; ball-and-socket, gliding, hinge, and pivot joints are different types of freely movable joints.

humerus   the bone of your upper arm.

intercostal muscles   small muscles between the ribs.

involuntary (or smooth) muscle   the type of muscle found in the internal organs.

large intestine   part of the digestive tract that moves waste products out of the body.

ligaments   tough, stringy bands of tissue that support and strengthen joints.

marrow   soft, fleshy tissue in the hollow of bones.

metatarsals   the bones in the middle part of your foot.

muscle fibers   thread-shaped cells that make up voluntary muscle.

osteoarthritis   inflammation on worn joints, causing pain and stiffness.

patella   the kneecap.

pelvis   the bone formed by the hip bones and sacrum.

periosteum   a tough skin covering bones.

radius   the shorter of the two lower arm bones.

reflexes   automatic muscle movements controlled by the spinal cord.

sacrum   the wedge-shaped bone at the bottom of the spine made of five fused vertebrae.

scapula   the shoulder blade.

sinuses   air-filled hollows in some skull and face bones.

skeleton   the body's bony framework.

small intestine   part of the digestive tract in which food is digested.

spinal cord   the column of nerve fibers running to and from the brain down the middle of the backbone.

sternum   the breastbone.

stirrup bone   one of the three tiny bones in the middle ear.

sutures   the joints between your skull bones.

tarsals   the bones of the ankle and heel.

tendons   tough, stringy material joining muscle to bones.

tibia   the shinbone.

triceps   the muscle at the back of your upper arm.

trunk (torso)   the central part of your body, without the head, neck, arms, and legs.

ulna   the longer of the two lower arm bones.

vertebrae   the linked bones that make up your backbone.

voluntary (or skeletal or striated) muscle   the type of strong body muscle that attaches to your bones and allows you to move.

Index

mE.